W9-CPE-155

BIGGER THAN

me

KIDS EXPLORE PHILADELPHIA

by students from the

RUSSELL BYERS CHARTER SCHOOL
PHILADELPHIA, PA

Powerful Voices
for Kids™ Press

By Kids, For Kids

This book is dedicated to everyone who tried to achieve something bigger than themselves ...and persevered!

Powerful Voices for Kids™ Press - By Kids, For Kids
ISBN: 978-0-9897622-0-5

Text and illustrations copyright © 2013 Russell Byers Charter School.
All rights reserved, including the right of reproduction in whole or in part in any form.

Book production by We Love Children's Books; design by Desiree Rappa & photographs by Sally Lindsay.

For over 300 years, Philadelphia has been a place where big ideas make a difference. Ideas of **freedom, democracy, education** and **good citizenship** all have deep roots here.

Our founding fathers were a team of **big thinkers** who believed we all have the right to life, liberty and the pursuit of happiness.

Without freedom and equality for all, none of us would be able to express our big ideas or pursue our dreams.

In my neighborhood there are a lot of things **bigger than me.** At my school I am learning about the importance of **big ideas.**

Behind every big idea

is a person or group that

thinks deeply.

William Penn was a
big thinker.
He founded Pennsylvania
and designed Philadelphia.

Big thinkers are still at work here, helping the city grow. They do things **no one has done before,** like building the tallest skyscraper in the city.

Benjamin Franklin was an author, scientist, diplomat and inventor. He had lots of **big ideas.**

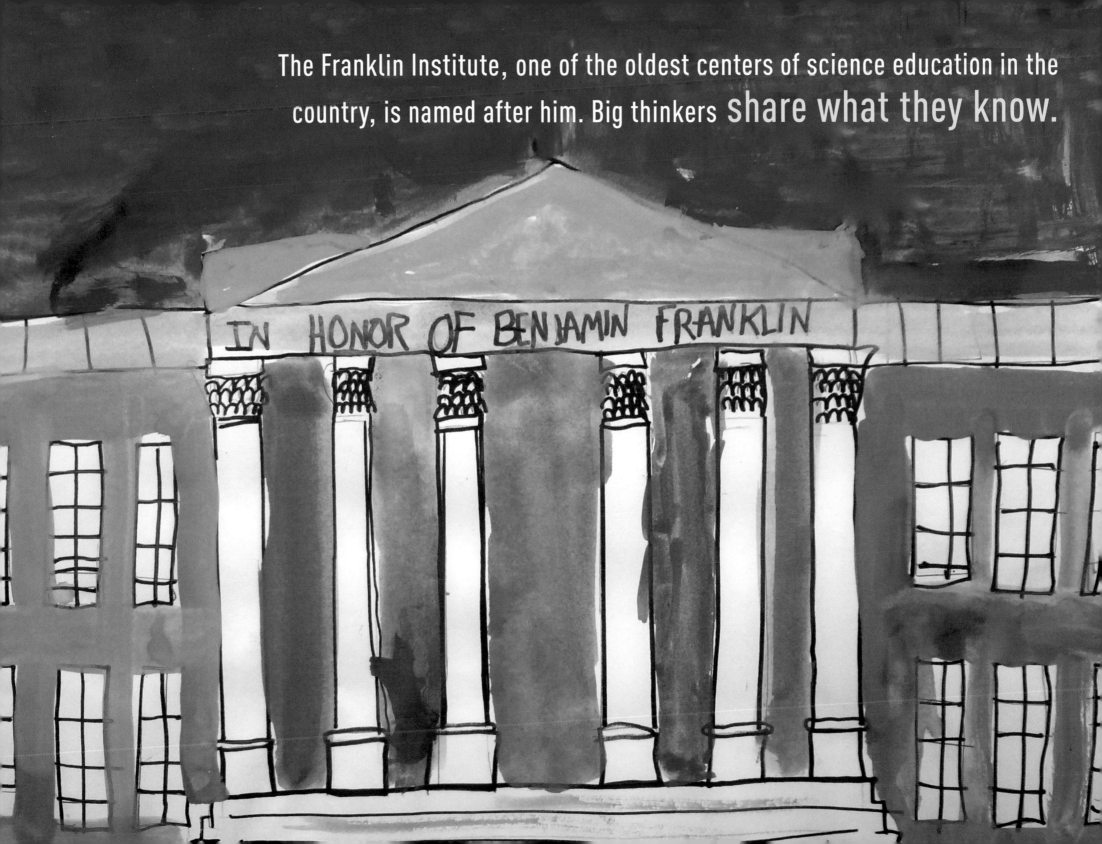

The Franklin Institute, one of the oldest centers of science education in the country, is named after him. Big thinkers share what they know.

Some scientists create technology that shapes the future.

Other scientists study the past to help us understand **where we came from.**
Big thinkers use their ideas to help us **discover** who we are and where we are going.

John Wanamaker was
a businessman who had
big ideas.
He built a store that
changed the way
people shop.

Architects design buildings that change the way we live. Big ideas get bigger when they **impact people's lives** every day.

Philadelphia has the oldest museum and art school in America. When it was founded, the Pennsylvania Academy of the Fine Arts was a **brand-new big idea,** especially in a young country.

Artists are big thinkers, too.
They **create things**
that most people could
never imagine.

Engineers and architects had a vision to build the first suspension bridge connecting Philadelphia to New Jersey. The Ben Franklin Bridge is still in use today.

That is some big idea!

It takes big ideas to plan a city. William Penn's original plan for Philadelphia included parks. Today, Philadelphia's Fairmount Park is the largest city park in the United States!

Big thinkers built Memorial Hall in Fairmount Park. Now it is the home of the Please Touch Museum, a place where children can have fun and begin to **think big.**

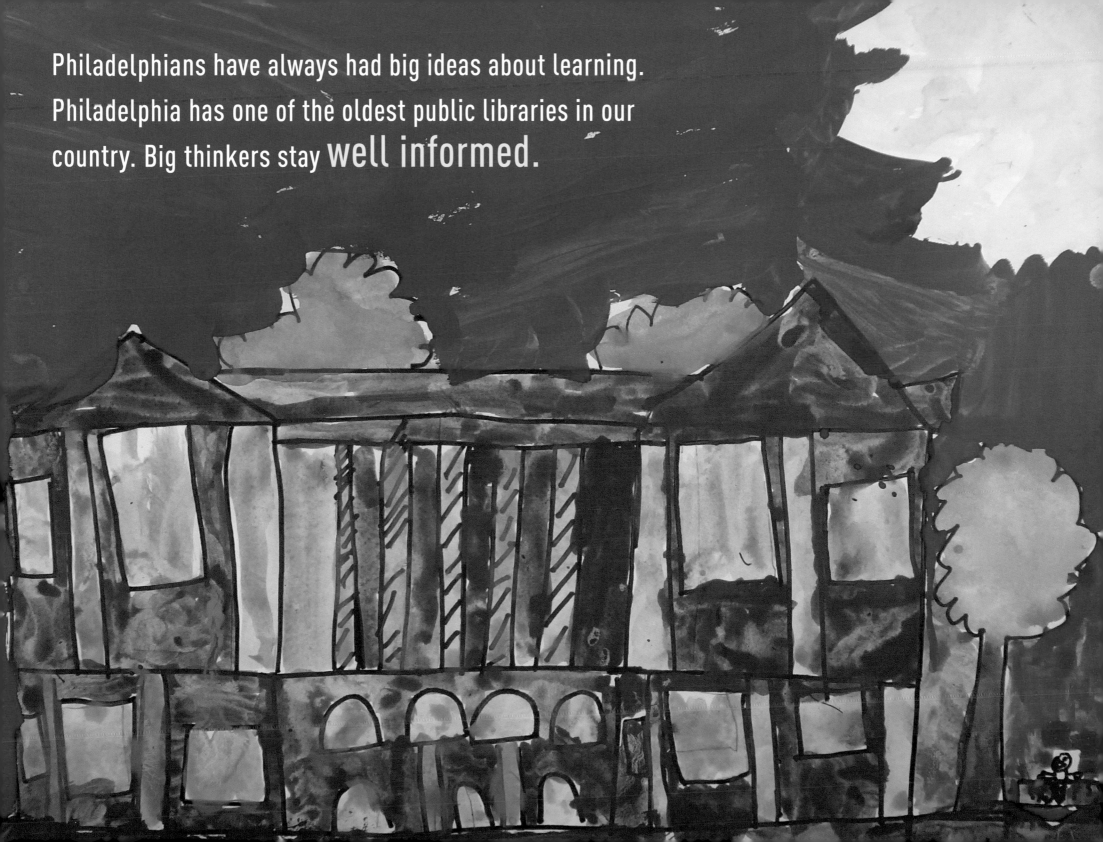

Philadelphians have always had big ideas about learning. Philadelphia has one of the oldest public libraries in our country. Big thinkers stay well informed.

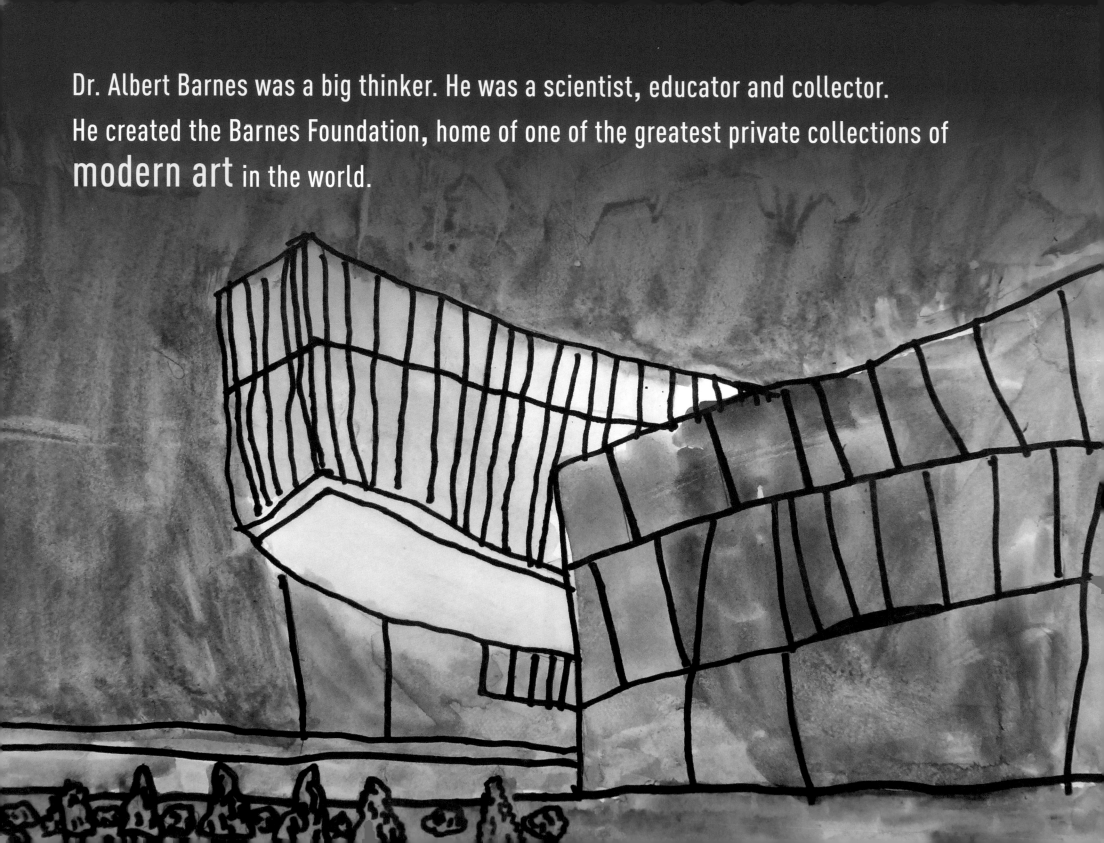

Dr. Albert Barnes was a big thinker. He was a scientist, educator and collector.
He created the Barnes Foundation, home of one of the greatest private collections of **modern art** in the world.

The Barnes Totem and reflecting pool remind
me that big thinkers take **time to reflect.**

The Philadelphia Museum of Art is filled with big ideas. It is a place of inspiration and contemplation.

The sculptures perched on top of the Art Museum are griffins. In legends, these creatures were the **guardians of treasures**. Big thinkers value, protect and champion the things that make our city special.

Philadelphia is full of **champions** that make our city great. Champions and **big thinkers** can be found everywhere. All of them **think big** and **dream even bigger.**

So I am thinking big, too. I am dreaming. I am imagining. I am planning. I will be part of something bigger than me.

 **ABOUT**

PHILADELPHIA

MORE ABOUT THE PLACES IN THIS BOOK

LOVE Park
(official name: JFK Plaza)

1965 | Architect: Vincent G. Kling
1976 | Sculptor: Robert Indiana

Originally famous for its Robert Indiana LOVE sculpture, skateboarders discovered that the combination of ramps, walls and steps made this park perfect for tricks! For years it was a destination for the best skaters and skateboarders in the world, but now it is illegal to skateboard there. You can still try it out in some skateboarding videogames.

Skyline of Philadelphia

For years there was an informal agreement not to build anything higher than the top of the statue of William Penn on City Hall (548 ft)—and that building stood as the city's tallest for 86 years. The completion of One Liberty Place (945 ft) in 1987 changed everything, and big buildings really took off! Right now, the tallest building in the city is the 57-story Comcast Center (974 ft). Philadelphia's skyline is one of the tallest in the nation. It is one of only 4 cities in the country to have two or more buildings over 900 feet.

Independence Hall

1748 | Architect: Edmund Woolley

Independence Hall was the site of many important moments during the founding of our nation. The Declaration of Independence was signed here, the first flag was unveiled, and our Constitution was drafted—all in this same historic building! Today, visitors to Independence Hall can see the copy of the Declaration of Independence that was read for the first time in public on July 8, 1776. Though the building looks much as it did back then, all the furniture has been replaced. In 1778, occupying British troops used the original furniture for firewood!

Liberty Bell

1752 | Whitechapel Bell Foundry, London

The Liberty Bell is a symbol of our nation's independence and the Revolutionary War. But did you know that the crack we see today is not its first? The very first time the bell rang, it cracked. Local workers repaired it—but now the bell sounded terrible! They fixed it again and in June of 1753 it was hung in the steeple of Independence Hall. But, 50 years later the bell was cracking again. The crack we see today happened in 1846 when the bell rang in honor of the birthday of George Washington.

Russell Byers Charter School

2001 | Founded in honor of slain *Philadelphia Daily News* columnist Russell Byers

At the Russell Byers Charter School, students learn by doing. Academic goals are linked to adventure, service work, teamwork, and character development. Each year RBCS 6th graders step out of their comfort zones to rappel off of the school building— three stories from the roof to the ground, supported only by ropes! Can you imagine doing that at your school?

Photo Credit: Ryan Brandenberg

The Thinker at the Rodin Museum

1929 | Architect: Paul Philippe Cret
First Casting: 1904 | Sculptor: Auguste Rodin

Auguste Rodin's The Thinker is one of the most famous sculptures in history. It is often used to represent philosophy—and shows a man thinking big thoughts! The first bronze casting of The Thinker is at Le Museé Rodin in Paris, France. Like most sculptors who work in bronze, Rodin made many castings of his statues. Philadelphia's casting of The Thinker is part of the Rodin Museum, which has the largest collection of the artist's work outside of Paris.

William Penn Statue atop Philadelphia City Hall

(see also: Philadelphia Skyline)

1901 | Architect: John McArthur
1892 | Sculptor: Alexander Milne Calder

Philadelphia City Hall is the largest and tallest city hall in the United States. It took so long to complete —30 years!—that when it was done the design was so out of fashion some people wanted to tear it down! Fortunately, it was too well constructed to be demolished cheaply and easily. Did you know you can go to the top of the building? There is an observation deck just below William Penn's statue that goes all the way around the building, providing a spectacular bird's eye view of the city. And of course, at the very top is the statue of William Penn, the founder of Philadelphia and Pennsylvania. The statue of William Penn used to be dressed up to bring luck to Philadelphia sports teams contending for championships, but it seemed to have the opposite effect. No matter how many times they dressed the statue up, the teams lost! When the Phillies reached the World Series in 2008, the city did not dress up the statue and the Phillies won!

Comcast Center

(see also: Philadelphia Skyline)
2008 | Architect: Robert A.M. Stern

The Comcast Center is the tallest building in Philadelphia, and is also the tallest "green" building in the country. It uses 40% less water than a typical office building. It also houses a 2000-square-foot LED screen with five times the resolution of a high-definition television which displays video and pictures 24 feet tall. But the most beloved part of this building is much smaller—the miniature statue of William Penn welded to the structure's highest point! Many people feel it broke the Curse of William Penn and brought Philadelphia the World Series victory in 2008.

Benjamin Franklin National Memorial

1938 | Architect: John T. Windrim
1911 | Sculptor: James Earle Fraser

The Franklin Institute in Philadelphia houses the official memorial to Benjamin Franklin. The centerpiece of the Benjamin Franklin National Memorial is a 20-foot high marble statue that took Fraser five years to complete. Originally opened in 1938, the Memorial is modeled after the Pantheon in Rome. The entire rotunda is made of different types of marble imported from Portugal, Italy, and France. Forming the entryway to the Franklin Institute, the rotunda and statue form a fitting tribute to one of our Founding Fathers, a man whose common sense and love of learning are immortalized in the institutions he helped to create.

The Franklin Institute

1934 | Architect: John T. Windrim

The Franklin Institute of the State of Pennsylvania for the Promotion of the Mechanic Arts was founded in 1824 to honor Benjamin Franklin and to further advance the usefulness of his inventions. In 1934, The Franklin Institute opened its Science Museum to the public. The exhibits are designed to help guests fall in love with the world of science through hands-on experiences. One of the most popular attractions is the Giant Walk-Through Heart. The Heart was originally planned as a temporary exhibit, to last only six months. People loved it so much, it has stayed open for over 50 years! How giant is it? It would fit comfortably into a 220-foot tall person.

Airplane Installation at The Franklin Institute

1934 | Architect: John T. Windrim
1931 | Manufacturer: Edward G. Budd Company

The Budd BB-1 Pioneer was an experimental flying boat—that means it could take off and land on water. It was built in the 1930s and was the first plane ever built of stainless steel! However, at the time, stainless steel was not considered practical, and only one BB-1 was built. After it toured the world, it was installed in front of the Franklin Institute in 1935 and has stayed there ever since. This is just one of the great attractions that The Franklin Institute has for flight enthusiasts, from the Wright Brothers all the way through space travel!

Dinosaur Sculpture at the Academy of Natural Sciences

1876 | Architect: James Hamilton Windrim
1987 | Sculptor: Kent Ullberg

If you like dinosaurs, thank the Academy of Natural Sciences! The man who discovered the first-ever dinosaur fossils was Joseph Leidy, a scientist with the Academy. He found dinosaur teeth in Montana back in 1856. The dinosaur sculpture in front of the building depicts *Deinonychus antirrhopus*, which lived 100 million years ago in the Cretaceous Period. Dinosaurs are one of the biggest attractions at the Academy—both in size and in popularity!

The Eagle at the Wanamaker Building

(now Macy's)
1911 | Architect: Daniel H. Burnham
1904 | Sculptor: August Gaul

Wanamaker's department store was the first department store in Philadelphia, and one of the first in the whole United States! The Wanamaker Eagle was created for the St. Louis World's Fair in 1904. It is bronze, stands 10 feet tall, weighs almost two and a half tons and has 5,000 customized feathers. It is so massive that the floor had to be reinforced just to support it! The large bronze eagle became the symbol of the store and is still a favorite meeting place for shoppers. If you tell your friends, "Let's meet at The Eagle," everyone will know what you mean.

PSFS Skyscraper

(now Loews Philadelphia Hotel)
1932 | Architects: William Lescaze, George Howe

When the Philadelphia Savings Fund Society building was completed in 1932, it was recognized around the world as a breakthrough architectural achievement. It was the first skyscraper in the United States built in the International style. This style of architecture uses very simple shapes and designs, creating a functional building, not one covered with decorations. The building also had many modern conveniences we take for granted today—like air conditioning! It was the first skyscraper to be air-conditioned throughout the year.

Paint Torch Sculpture at the Pennsylvania Academy of the Fine Arts

1876 | Architects: Frank Furness, George W. Hewitt
2011 | Sculptor: Claes Oldenburg

Founded in 1805, the Pennsylvania Academy of the Fine Arts is the nation's oldest art museum and school. It is also the home of another fun outdoor sculpture—the Paint Torch. The 51-foot tall, illuminated, blue-and-orange paint brush is positioned so it looks as if it is in the act of painting. This piece pays tribute to all painters, both masters and students, as well as to the Academy itself as a beacon of culture.

Scullers on the Schuylkill River at Fairmount Park

Fairmount Park is the largest landscaped city park in the United States—even bigger than New York's Central Park! It stretches along the Schuylkill River from the Art Museum to Forbidden Drive and beyond! At the south end of the Schuylkill stands Boathouse Row, home to the famous scullers, immortalized in the paintings of Thomas Eakins and others for over a hundred years. The river and Boathouse Row have combined to make Philadelphia one of the most important places for rowing in the United States. At night, Boathouse Row is all lit up with twinkling lights!

Clothespin Sculpture

1976 | Sculptor: Claes Oldenburg

Did you know Philadelphia has more public art than any other city in America? It's everywhere you look. In fact, across the street from City Hall, towering over a subway entrance, you can see a giant clothespin! This 45-foot-high, 10-ton sculpture stops visitors in their tracks. Claes Oldenburg related his Clothespin sculpture to Constantin Brancusi's famous sculpture The Kiss, which is at the Philadelphia Museum of Art. Can you see two people embracing in the Clothespin's shape?

Please Touch Museum at Memorial Hall

1876 | Architect: Hermann J. Schwarzmann

Memorial Hall was built in 1876 for the Centennial Exhibition, America's first World's Fair. It went through many changes, including being the first Art Museum, and even a police station! In 2008, Memorial Hall became the home of Philadelphia's Please Touch Museum. The Please Touch Museum was the first of its kind in the nation. It encouraged younger children to explore and to play with the exhibits—unlike other museums where visitors are told, "Please DO NOT Touch!"

Benjamin Franklin Bridge

1926 | Architect: Paul Philippe Cret

The Benjamin Franklin Bridge is one of the world's largest suspension bridges. It connects Philadelphia, PA to Camden, NJ. Look for the towers on either end of the bridge. These are known as "anchorages," the places where the suspension cables are anchored to the ground. These anchorages were originally designed to be passenger stations for trolley lines. They are decorated inside and very beautiful.

Free Library of Philadelphia

1927 | Architect: Julian F. Abele

The Central Branch of the Free Library of Philadelphia opened in 1927. It contains more than 7 million items and many special collections. That is quite a difference from its first home—three cramped rooms in City Hall! When Dr. William Pepper founded the Library in 1891, there were private libraries in the city, which people had to pay to use. Dr. Pepper declared, "This is the People's Library, absolutely free to all!" This was reflected by the library's first motto: "Liber Libere Omnibus"— Free Books for All!

Photo Credit: The Barnes Foundation

The Barnes Foundation

2012 | Architects: Tod Williams, Billie Tsien

The art collection assembled by Dr. Albert C. Barnes is one of the greatest in the world. He did not collect works from just a single time period or style, nor did he display them in a traditional way. He built his own museum where he organized his collection the way he wanted to. Unlike most museums, the galleries were organized by composition, color and the relationship of one piece of art to the next. Now located along the Benjamin Franklin Parkway, the Barnes Foundation still displays the pictures exactly as Dr. Barnes originally arranged them. Going to the Barnes Foundation is not like visiting any other museum. . . and that's the way Dr. Barnes wanted it!

The Barnes Totem and Reflecting Pool

2012 | Sculptor: Ellsworth Kelly

The Barnes Totem stands tall at the head of a long reflecting pool lined with red maples outside the Barnes Foundation. The 40-foot-high sculpture works with its surroundings to focus and heighten visitors' sense of being in a special place. Though the piece is deceptively simple many considerations went into creating and installing it: Where should its stepped element be located? What direction should it point? Once the piece was finished the sculptor worked with the building and landscape architects to select the place where it now stands. What's it supposed to be? That's up to you! It isn't meant to look like any one thing; it is supposed to make you think and feel something different each time.

Philadelphia Museum of Art

1928 | Architects: Horace Trumbauer; Zantzinger, Borie, and Medary

The Philadelphia Museum of Art is one of the most awe-inspiring places in the country. Julian Francis Abele, the first African-American architect to gain professional acclaim, helped develop the design of the building based on the temples of Ancient Greece, placing the building atop a hill known as the Faire Mount—where Fairmount Park gets its name. The Museum overlooks the city from its vantage point at the end of the Benjamin Franklin Parkway, exactly one mile from City Hall. This museum is one of the largest in the country, with exhibits that span two thousand years and cover six continents.

Griffin Sculptures atop Philadelphia Museum of Art

1928 | Sculptor: C. Paul Jennewein

The griffin is a mythical creature with the head and wings of an eagle and the body of a lion. It is also the symbol of the Philadelphia Museum of Art! In ancient times, these powerful, majestic creatures were said to guard treasures and priceless possessions. The Art Museum building is adorned by a collection of bronze griffins—they are perched on each corner of the museum and "protect" the treasures found within.

Rocky Statue

1980 | Sculptor: A. Thomas Schomberg

In front of the Philadelphia Museum of Art stands the Rocky statue made famous by Sylvester Stallone's iconic Rocky films. Visiting the statue and recreating Rocky's triumphant run up the Art Museum steps is one of the most popular things to do when visiting the city. Like Sylvester Stallone's character in the films, you can run up the 72 steps that lead to the front entrance of the museum, punching the air in victory. Find the imprint of Rocky's feet at the top of the steps and take a look down the Benjamin Franklin Parkway to the Philadelphia skyline. That's some view!

Cathedral Basilica of Saints Peter and Paul

1864 | Architect: Napoleon LeBrun

LeBrun designed this cathedral when he was only 25 years old. He was concerned about possible vandalism, so originally the cathedral had no windows at street level—it only had windows high up in the walls, called clerestory windows. People say that the architect and construction workers threw rocks as high as they could to figure out where to put the windows.

This book is the result of a first through sixth grade case study of Philadelphia landmarks, envisioned by visual arts teacher Amy Jared. The Russell Byers Charter School is an incubator, a hotbed of curiosity and inquiry, a center of investigation and exploration, a portal to our city...and the world! It is a place where children believe **"I can"** instead of "I can't."

MEET THE ARTISTS

LOVE Park (title page)
Jayln Clark, Sixth Grade

Russell Byers Charter School (dedication page)
Tyree Petteway, Third Grade

Skyline of Philadelphia
Grace Maroon, Second Grade

Independence Hall
Makiya Adams, Second Grade

Liberty Bell
Caleb Tann, Sixth Grade

Russell Byers Charter School
Caitlin Ott, Third Grade

The Thinker at the Rodin Museum
Orlando Martinez, Sixth Grade

William Penn Statue atop Philadelphia City Hall
Mia Pagan, First Grade

Comcast Center
Sadon Powell, Sixth Grade

Benjamin Franklin National Memorial
Tyie Powell, Fifth Grade

The Franklin Institute
Adrian Boone, Fifth Grade

Airplane Installation at The Franklin Institute
Tyler Tolbert, Fifth Grade

Dinosaur Sculpture at the Academy of Natural Sciences
Caleb Jones, Sixth Grade

The Eagle at the Wanamaker Building
Jeremy Savage, Sixth Grade

PSFS Skyscraper
Cara Bucher, Second Grade

Paint Torch Sculpture at the Pennsylvania Academy of the Fine Arts
Tiffani Bundy, Sixth Grade

Clothespin Sculpture
Jabril Washington, Fifth Grade

Benjamin Franklin Bridge
Shane Holland, Fifth Grade

Scullers on the Schuylkill River at Fairmount Park
Kay-Cee Cuttino, Fifth Grade

Please Touch Museum at Memorial Hall
Najm Al-din Hameed, Fifth Grade

Free Library of Philadelphia
Jaedon Coleman, Third Grade

The Barnes Foundation
Kalina Kozlowski, Third Grade

Barnes Totem and Reflecting Pool
Deja Watts, Sixth Grade

Philadelphia Museum of Art
Levi Morton, Fifth Grade

Griffin Sculptures atop Philadelphia Museum of Art
Edward Basley, Sixth Grade

Rocky Statue
Brian Henderson, Sixth Grade

LOVE Sculpture
Destiny Sharpe, Sixth Grade

Cathedral Basilica of Saints Peter and Paul
Justin Pagan, Third Grade

PHILADELPHIA

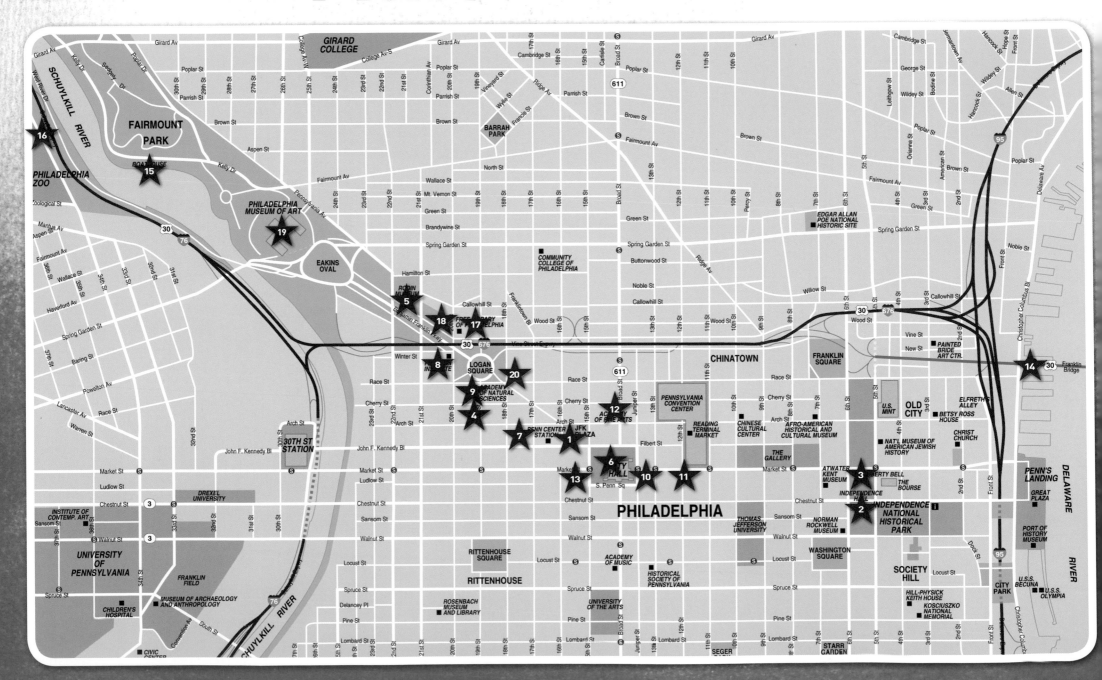

BIGGER THAN  me LANDMARKS

 1 LOVE Park (official name: JFK Plaza)

 2 Independence Hall

 3 Liberty Bell

 4 Russell Byers Charter School

 5 The Thinker at the Rodin Museum

 6 William Penn Statue atop Philadelphia City Hall

 7 Comcast Center

 8 The Franklin Institute/Benjamin Franklin National Memorial/Airplane Installation

 9 Dinosaur Sculpture at the Academy of Natural Sciences

 10 The Eagle at the Wanamaker Building (now Macy's)

 11 PSFS Skyscraper (now Loews Philadelphia Hotel)

 12 Paint Torch Sculpture at the Pennsylvania Academy of the Fine Arts

 13 Clothespin Sculpture

 14 Benjamin Franklin Bridge

 15 Boathouse Row: Scullers on the Schuylkill River at Fairmount Park

 16 Please Touch Museum at Memorial Hall

 17 Free Library of Philadelphia

 18 The Barnes Foundation/Barnes Totem and Reflecting Pool

 19 Philadelphia Museum of Art/Griffin Sculptures/ Rocky Statue

 20 Cathedral Basilica of Saints Peter and Paul

DRAW YOUR FAVORITE "BIGGER THAN ME" LANDMARK IN PHILADELPHIA. WHAT'S THE BIG IDEA BEHIND IT?